MONEY MANAGEMENT

for college students

MONEY for college students MANAGEMENT

LARRY BURKETT

with Todd Temple

MOODY PRESS

CHICAGO

All Scripture quotations are from the *New American Standard Bible*, © the Lockman Foundation 1960, 1962, 1963, 1968, 1971, 1972, 1973, 1975, 1977. Used by permission.

Edited by Adeline Griffith, Christian Financial Concepts
Project Coordinator, L. Allen Burkett
Contributing Researchers, Gordon Wadsworth and Michael McNeilly

Library of Congress Cataloging-in-Publication Data

Burkett, Larry.
    Money management for college students

ISBN#0-8024-6347-9
    1. College students—United States—Finance, Personal.
       Title.

5 7 9 10 8 6

Printed in the United States of America.

Contents

Introduction   7

Chapter 1   College Career Guidance   9

Chapter 2   College Financing   19

Chapter 3   Who Should Budget and Why   27

Chapter 4   Money Management 101   33

Chapter 5   Checkbook Management   45

Chapter 6   Credit Card Management   51

Chapter 7   Epilogue   57

Introduction

College orientation lectures should begin with, "Welcome to the world of high finance," because that's exactly what college is. As a college student, you're faced with decisions about school loans, credit cards, high book prices, and ever-escalating tuition costs. It's little wonder that college students and grads alike are having financial problems.

The financial aid officers usually point out that the student loans  don't have to be repaid until you're out of college. Instead, they should emphasize, "Now remember! These loans will have to be repaid—with interest— once you're out of college, irrespective of your income or other obligations."

Similarly, those credit card applications should come with a warning: "Danger! Acceptance and use of this card can, and will, jeopardize your college career and your marriage."

The ways to overspend today are a dazzling array. They include credit cards, school loans, automatic overdrafts, automatic tellers, car loans, even lunch charges in the school cafeteria. In order to avoid these pitfalls, you must be armed with *knowledge*. It constantly amazes me that so many young people get as far as college and, yet, have never taken a course on how to balance a checkbook or develop a budget. Since we all have to do those things, it seems to me that these, along with courses on how to buy cars, insurance policies, and homes, should be required for everyone.

You can study advance calculus or learn all there is to know about reading a corporate spreadsheet, but if you can't live on a budget and balance your own checkbook you're going to have a tough time in your marriage.

This workbook is dedicated to teaching you the practical financial tools you need to live in our society. But if we merely shared information we would be shortchanging you. With enough facts, I might be able to convince you to save some money for future needs (a lost art today). But, inevitably, some slick salesman would come along and convince you that he or she has *just* what you always needed; and down will go your savings! And usually plus some debt.

So, what Todd Temple and I are sharing in the workbook is not just information; it is wisdom—God's wisdom. The wisdom of God's Word has survived the Greeks, the Romans, all the kings and queens of Europe, and even the foolishness of the current generation.

God's truths are not complicated; they are simple and direct. Learn to apply them to your finances and you will be counted among the wise of our society, instead of one of the foolhardy.

Once you have completed this study, I heartily encourage you to help your college friends understand these principlesl.

Sincerely,

Larry Burkett

CHAPTER 1

College Career Guidance

Choosing a college and an appropriate major are important decisions with lasting financial implications. Frequently students feel stuck—not knowing where to turn or how to choose. Coupled with pressure from family, peers, and even the school, many blindly select a college and a major without praying about it first or without the benefit of a well-thought-out process. Often these impulsive choices result in changing majors, or schools, which can be very expensive.

Changing majors in college favorably compares to switching lines at the grocery store. You're free to make the switch, but you lose your position in line and generally have to start at the end of another line. How much wiser it is to make an informed choice in the first place.

To understand the process of choosing a college major, think of your four-year undergraduate studies in two phases. **Phase one** usually covers your first two years of studies and is heavily loaded with foundational courses that *everyone* has to take, regardless of their majors. These include classes in English, history, and mathematics. **Phase two** typically begins with your junior year, when most schools insist that you declare a college major field of study. Declaring your major narrows the focus of your studies and leads to a bachelors degree in a major area that usually relates to a specific career field. For instance, although a premed major and prelaw major will have the same required foundational courses in their first two years, their courses in the last two years of college will vary greatly. In the same way, courses for someone preparing to teach will be vastly different from someone preparing for a degree in veterinary science.

Suppose, at the end of a business major's junior year, he or she decides to switch majors to an education degree. Most of that student's junior year courses, preparing him or her for business studies, will not count toward a degree in education; therefore, the course credits are lost. Losing time and credits can be quite expensive, as seen in the example below.

As a result of changing majors twice during his undergraduate studies, it took John six years instead of four to obtain his bachelors degree, which resulted in the following impact on his personal finances.

The College Board estimated that the average expense of attending a four-year public college in 1995 was $9,300 per year, including tuition, room and board, books, fees, and incidentals. So John's two additional years, as a result of changing majors, added another $18,600 to the cost of his four year degree. But wait. There's more.

To understand the complete picture, you also must calculate the two years of salary that John *did not earn* because he was in school rather than working. Figuring an arbitrary, but modest, salary of $25,000 per year, John's extra two years cost him another $50,000 in *lost income*.

As a result, the total financial impact of his two additional years in college approached $68,600 (the cost of the additional college expenses *plus* two years of lost income because he was not working). That's quite a financial swing in a two-year period of time!

So you can see how tarrying in college can be very, very expensive. You've heard the saying that the shortest distance between two points is a straight line. Similarly, the shortest distance to graduation is to carefully select your college major. Of course, if you simply hate what you're studying, a change is both wise and necessary. But, in order to minimize changes, the trick is to accurately select a major in the first place.

How To Choose a College Major

The Life Pathways division of Christian Financial Concepts has helped thousands of high school and college students to select their major fields of study. I have listed below some of the most common mistakes people make in selecting a college major, followed by tips for making a wise choice.

Poor Reasons to Choose a College Major

1. Because the resulting job will make a lot of money.
Although finances are an important consideration in career planning (if not, we'd all be volunteers!), money should not be the sole factor in selecting a major and career. The Life Pathways staff has assisted a number of highly paid professionals, such as doctors, dentists, and attorneys, who weren't happy in their work because it didn't match their interests and personality.

2. Because it will lead to a "hot job."
First of all, a job that's "hot" today may not match your talents and interests. Second, the hot jobs of today may not be so hot by the time you get your degree, especially if post-graduate work is required. Indeed, one career counselor reported in *The Washington Times*: "Fifty percent of the jobs that will exist in the year 2005 haven't even been created yet."

3. Because it's the career field your parents specialized in.
It's likely that you will be more familiar with your parents' occupational fields than others, but that can't be the sole reason for choosing that same career track. You are uniquely created by God. What has been great for your parents may not suit you at all.

4. Because that's what your friends are pursuing.
Although there's some merit to choosing a college in order to stick with close friends, the selection of a college major must be distinctive to you and your skills, interests, and values.

Choosing a major by following the crowd is risky and may prove to be costly further into your academic career.

Wise Steps To Choosing a College Major
1. Wrestle with the purpose of your life.
Have you begun to formulate a mission statement for your life? Have you grappled with God's purpose for you? Those are profound, soul-searching questions that most people—adults included—struggle to understand. Easy answers to those questions are the exception rather than the rule. Yet, there is great value in the process of hammering out your personal mission statement in life.

2. To clarify your purpose, take inventory of your God-given talents.
Psalm 139:14 states that we are "fearfully and wonderfully made" by God. These unique God-given talents, blended with the particular people or events that have helped to shape us, such as family, educational, and social influences, provide the basis for sound career decisions. In His grace and wisdom, God provides talents, thus equipping us to accomplish His purpose in our lives. As stewards, our responsibility is to discover those talents and utilize them to His glory. You can take a major step toward understanding God's purpose for your life by discovering your God-given talents.

To arrive at a well-rounded understanding of your God-given talents, there are four primary factors to consider.

a. *Your personality.* Some enjoy solving people problems; others prefer to solve problems that relate to things, data, or ideas. Some enjoy taking initiative in the work setting; others prefer to follow the lead. Insights into your God-given personality will help you to understand the kinds of work you are best suited for, thus leading to wise choices of college majors and careers.

b. *Your skills.* Some naturally work well with their hands; others work best with analytical processes. The competitive edge in the workplace belongs to the person who can match skill development with natural talents.

c. *Vocational interests.* People typically excel in their work if their hearts are naturally motivated toward the activities associated with it. Make sure you do something you love. The more vocational interests you discover, the more possibilities you'll have to choose from. For this reason, it's wise to spend your high school and early college years just becoming exposed to a variety of occupational fields, thus broadening your base of interests and gaining insights into what you really like and don't like.

d. *Work priorities and values.* Some people place a high priority on working outdoors where they can have lots of fresh air, mobility, and independence; other people value working nine-to-five in a clean, office environment. In addition, core life values, such as achievement, recognition, financial gain, and serving God, compete with one another in your decision-making processes. Can you identify the core values that are influencing your approach to work?

Staying focused on such a self-examination is no easy task. To assist you, Life Pathways offers a comprehensive career assessment that will highlight your personality strengths (and weaknesses), vocational interests, skills, and values. Included in the modest testing fee are helpful support materials, such as the 180-page workbook, *Guide to College Majors and Career Choices.* For more information about Career Pathways, call the ministries of Christian Financial Concepts at 1-800-722-1976.

3. Consider the high school subject areas you found most appealing.

Another important clue to the selection of your college major can be found in your previous educational experiences. For instance, if you loved journalism and English, carefully review your college catalog for available courses in these areas. On the other hand, if you struggled with these subjects or had a hard time maintaining interest in them, you probably won't want to pursue a degree in these fields.

After you have considered each of these factors, try to identify a few general career fields in which your personality, interests, skills, and values overlap. With some possibilities in view, determine the college majors that will prepare you for those career fields.

To help you, study the course selections and majors in a college catalog. Is your interest aroused as you read the course descriptions? Consider the skills that will be necessary to succeed both in the college major and in the related career fields. Taking this step may force you to think consistently about your talents, interests, courses of study, and career fields.

In addition to reviewing the college catalog, there are some more steps you can take to match college majors to potential career fields.

- **Talk to college professors or high school teachers in the field.**
- **Talk to college seniors who are majoring in the subject.**
- **Talk to business professionals (especially members of your church) in the career fields you are considering.**
- **Join or visit a campus group related to the career fields you're interested in.**
- **Study professional journals and publications in the library.**

Choosing a College

After you have selected a major, you can begin the process of choosing your school. The choices number in the thousands, including Christian colleges, community colleges, technical schools, private colleges, and public universities. Your career plans will narrow the list dramatically, and your SATs, GPA, and finances may trim it even more.

When evaluating possible choices, take the following factors into account.

✔ **Academic competitiveness of the school.** In light of your scholastic ability, do you stand a good chance of being admitted?

✔ **Strength in your academic major.** Does the school excel in the areas of your academic interests?

✔ **Urban versus rural.** Do you want to attend college in a city or in a rural setting?

✔ **Proximity to home.** How important is it for you to be close to home?

✔ **Class size.** Can you handle university classes with hundreds of students, or will you do better in smaller classes?

✔ **Cost.** What will you realistically be able to afford?

✔ **Christian versus secular.** Can your personal faith withstand the humanistic, politically correct bent of a secular school?

✔ **Safety.** How safe is the school's campus?

✔ **Residence.** Will you be required to live on campus?

✔ **Graduate placement.** What assistance does the school offer to graduating seniors?

✔ **Specialty programs.** If you are interested in special programs such as ROTC or ties to a special research program, be sure they're available.

✔ **Tradition and family ties.** Do you have family ties to the school? Did your parents or grandparents graduate from there?

Although this is not an exhaustive list of factors, it will help you to identify key elements in your selection of schools. Consider also the different types of educational institutions, as well as how each might best serve your purposes. Each has its benefits and disadvantages The following are a few types for you to think about.

Types of Schools

1. State Universities offer a broad range of courses and majors. Unlike many smaller schools, they have strong funding for staff, equipment, and other educational and recreational resources. Larger campuses also offer a diverse mix of social, professional, and religious organizations and groups.

2. Two-year community colleges offer advantages that aren't available from other schools. Many students attend to prepare for a career that requires a two-year degree. Others use a community college as a cost effective "proving-ground" before moving on to a four-year college. There they can adjust to college life, improve their grades, work part-time to save money, or delay the step of declaring a major.

3. Christian colleges can provide a solid education in a Christian environment presented from a Christian worldview.

You should strongly consider the lifelong value of having a Christian-based education as you prepare for your life and work. In addition, Christian colleges can offer courses and majors that aren't available at other schools, such as Christian education, youth ministry, theology, missions, and many others. Some denominationally affiliated schools offer scholarships to students from their churches.

4. Vocational and technical schools offer diploma programs for a variety of business, industrial, and health-care professions. Students in these programs get valuable, hands-on experience, often with the help of those already working in the field, including those who may consider employing them. Because many of their students are already working or still deciding on a career field, vo-tech schools offer flexible hours, quicker programs, and enrollments staggered throughout the year.

Grades on a transcript are permanent and will stand as your record of commitment and achievement.

College Decision Checklist

_____ I have taken the SAT/ACT.

_____ I have considered my unique blend of skills, interests, personality traits, and values.

_____ I have discussed my plans with my parents and/or guidance counselor.

_____ I have talked with graduates or friends who have attended the colleges I am considering.

_____ I have explored the majors offered at various schools.

_____ I have investigated different plans for financing my college education and have made a financial plan.

_____ I have taken steps to begin exploring college majors.

_____ I have reviewed college catalogs of several schools I am considering.

_____ I have visited the campus of several colleges I am considering.

_____ I have sent applications for enrollment, official high school or college transcripts, and SAT/ACT scores to the colleges I am considering.

_____ I have determined my living arrangements at college.

_____ I have set GPA goals and made a strong commitment to be a good student in college and thus get the benefits of my education.

CHAPTER 2

College Financing

It's no secret that college tuitions continue to rise at a rate that is faster than inflation. One analyst predicts that in a few years the average state school, which is heavily subsidized, could cost as much as $6,000 to 8,000 per year for tuition alone. To that add room and board, books, and all the other expenses, and you may be paying $60,000 for your diploma.

Because the cost of higher education has increased so drastically during the last few years, most students and their families cannot afford to pay for college without financial help. College financial assistance comes in three forms: scholarships, grants, and student loans. Let's look at each of these sources of money.

Scholarships

Many people I talk to have the mistaken idea that there are piles of unclaimed scholarship money out there just waiting to be grabbed. The unused-scholarship myth is an old one. As long as there are so-called scholarship search firms picking up $50 to $150 to find scholarships for prospective students, the myth will be perpetuated. Here are the facts.

SCHOLARSHIP TIPS

When searching for available scholarships, keep these tips in mind.

- **Disregard the unclaimed scholarships myth.**
- **Ask a lot of questions; challenge promises.**
- **Get everything in writing.**
- **Weigh the odds before writing innumerable essays.**
- **Avoid college-fund gimmicks from insurance companies.**
- **Avoid scholarship search firms.**

Merit-based scholarships are awarded to students with high academic performance, artistic talent, or athletic ability. Some scholarships are provisional: If you fail to live up to the requirements, you must repay them. For example, some medical school scholarships come with the provision that you must practice in a rural area after graduation. If you fail to live up to your end of the bargain, you may get stuck with a repayment obligation three times the amount of the scholarship.

Some college scholarships come from private foundations and organizations: chambers of commerce, service groups, church denominations, foundations, corporations, civic clubs, alumni associations, professional associations, and trade unions. Ask your high school guidance counselor, teachers, pastor, and other community leaders about what's available. Most high schools and colleges now have computer access to lists of financial aid sources, including scholarships.

Colleges and universities often have their own scholarships, which they use to recruit and reward superior students. Athletic scholarships get lots of attention in the press, but schools recruit academic talent too. Check with the college financial aid office for information and applications for these scholarships.

Students who take the PSAT/NMSQT (National Merit Scholarship Qualifying Test) as a high school sophomore or junior may qualify for the National Merit Scholarship. For more information, write PSAT/NMSQT, 1560 Sherman Ave Ste 200, Evanston, IL 60201-4897.

Grants

Federal and state grants for college education are available to students who have a great financial need. Like most scholarships, grant funds do not need to be repaid when you graduate. One such program is called the Pell Grant, which is available directly from the federal government to qualified undergraduates who can show a financial need. Another federal program is the Supplemental Educational Opportunity Grant, which is administered by the school.

The College Work-Study program (CWS) is a grant you work for. The college teams up with the federal or state government to provide money for your education. In turn, the college sets you up with an on-campus or off-campus job, sometimes in your field of study. Instead of paying you with a paycheck, the school pays you with an education.

Loans

In the 1980s the federal government responded to the rising costs of higher education by making it easier for students and their families to qualify and repay loans. They did this by offering low-interest loans of their own and offering to guarantee the loans of other institutions who lend to students.

The good news is that many more students can now afford to get a diploma. The bad news is that most of those students will be in financial bondage for years after graduation, while they try to pay off their loans.

The Perkins Loan program lends federal money to needy students through their schools. In other programs, such as the Stafford Loan, the money actually comes from private institutions, such as banks, but the loan is guaranteed by the government.

Federally guaranteed loans essentially make Uncle Sam the cosigner on a loan made by a bank or other financial institution. If you default on the loan, "we the people of the United States" pay back the lender. Of course, the lender will still hound you to repay the loan so it can lend this money to the next student. And don't forget that your payments—or lack of them—leave a lasting mark on your young credit report.

The Perkins Loan and the Stafford Loan are need-based. This means that you must show a financial need in order to qualify. Other loans, such as the Parent Loan for Undergraduate Students (PLUS), have no need requirement. Even if you and your family have no need to borrow, these programs will let you do it anyway—as long as you've already applied for need-based loans.

With all of these loans available, it's tempting just to pay for your education with borrowed money and worry about the repayment later. To keep enrollments up, colleges have streamlined the complicated financial aid process, making it relatively simple for you to sign away a huge chunk of your future income. They *want* you in school, paying tuition, paying their bills, keeping the school in business. Where the tuition money comes from is not a big concern to them, as long as it's paid. So *you* must be the one who guards your future. *You* must make sure that the financial aid help they're offering is best for you in the long run.

It's not easy to avoid the temptation of low-interest loans. Most people figure they'll be making lots of money after they graduate, and the monthly loan payments won't amount to much. And most of those folks learn that they figured wrong.

An annual salary of $20,000, $30,000, or $40,000 seems like a lot of cash when you've been working minimum-wage jobs till now. But chances are, you've been living on a subsidy called *Parents,* who pay the rent, fill the fridge, finance your braces, and keep you in clothes. But that subsidy soon ends, and all those bills will take a colossal chunk out of that seemingly large salary. When you stick a loan payment on top of it all, there may be nothing left, and you may find yourself longing for those subsidized days of minimum wage. I know of brilliant, hardworking adults in their thirties who are *still* paying off their college loans. There's got to be a better way.

There is. It's still possible to graduate from a good college, with a good education, without a heavy debt to haunt you. Here are some ideas.

Alternative Funding Ideas

Over the years, I have heard of many different plans for getting through school without having to mortgage an arm and a leg. The most economical plan is one of the most popular: Live at home, attend an inexpensive community college for one or two years, and work part-time to save up money until you transfer to a four-year school. This may seem unappealing or unimpressive to some students. But four years later, those who carefully follow this plan graduate with the same diploma as their peers, and they do so with a lot less debt to tie them down after graduation.

Some students join the co-op program in their second year of college. This normally adds only one year to the total time it takes to earn a bachelor's degree, but it also adds approximately $8,000 a year in student income. Most universities have special departments that will give you the details. In essence, it means going to school one quarter, working the next. This program can provide valuable on-the-job experience—and it looks great on a resúmé.

The military offers money-earning opportunities for college students. If you join a reserve unit in the Army, Navy, Air Force, Marines, or Coast Guard, or enlist in the Air or Army National Guard, you'll be paid over $100 a month to attend a weekend drill; plus they'll drop another $190 in your lap every month you remain in school. And you pick up extra cash for training in the summer. Also, if you join the ROTC at your college as a junior, you'll get another $100 each month and return to your reserve unit as an officer when you graduate.

If you plan to enter government service in the military, law enforcement, or the Peace Corps, or you plan to become a teacher to students in low-income areas, you may want to consider the federal Perkins Loan program. Students who enter certain government agencies after graduation don't have to repay the loan.

The Financial Aid Process

The federal government, your state government, and your

school offer many forms of financial aid, and the eligibility and application process for each of these sources varies. The best thing to do is to pick up a packet of financial aid information at the school you wish to attend. This packet contains information, worksheets, applications, and a list of all the deadlines you'll need to know.

To make the complicated financial aid process easier, you can apply for most grants and loans using the same application form, called the Free Application for Federal Student Aid (FAFSA). It's available at the school's financial aid office. The FAFSA asks all sorts of questions about you and your family's finances; the government uses this information to determine which grants and loans you're eligible for.

Basically, the government uses the numbers you put down on your FAFSA to come up with a figure called the EFC, or Expected Family Contribution. This is the amount of money they figure you and your folks can afford to contribute to your education. If the EFC is less than the cost of tuition, books, and living expenses, the government and your school then point you to grants and loans that make up the difference.

Let's say that your family has an EFC of $4,000 and your school says that the cost of attending is $3,800 a year. You have no need for financial aid. That's great news! You can afford to attend school debt-free. If the cost of your education is $9,000 a year, then you'll be eligible for $5,000 a year in grants and low-interest loans.

As I said, the government uses your family's tax forms and other information you provide on the FAFSA to figure out your EFC. Some students and their families are tempted to fudge the numbers on these forms to make themselves eligible for grants and low-interest loans. But "fudging" is just a polite word for cheating, and "government" is merely a fancy word for us. In other words, "we the people" are the ones being cheated. Honest, hardworking taxpayers fund those grants and subsidize the interest on these loans. *Somebody* has to work to pay for your education. Do your honest best to pay for it yourself.

Your FAFSA must be submitted no earlier than January 1 of the calendar year you plan to start school. That's because it asks questions about your family's previous tax year, which won't be over until then. Some states have financial aid programs that require your completion of this form as early as March 1, so you should submit it as soon after January 1 as possible. It's a good incentive to get your parents to do their taxes early.

By the way, if you're no longer a dependent living at home, you can still use the FAFSA to apply for financial aid. In this case, you can complete the form without your parents' financial information. The application explains how to determine if you're "independent" in the eyes of the government, and how to complete the form if you are.

The financial aid process is complicated. It's essential that you get all the information you need, as soon as you can. Read *everything*—it will be good practice for college! No one expects you to become an expert in all the written information, so ask questions if something isn't clear. Your high school guidance counselor and the school's financial aid office staff are paid to help you.

Mark all deadlines in your calendar so you don't miss important application dates. And make sure you fill out every application accurately; the offices that process them have hundreds or thousands to shuffle, and they routinely send back anything that's not done right.

Finding a way to pay for college is complicated, but it's not impossible. Remember, with diligent effort and prayer there *is* a way. When Hitler had conquered most of Europe and turned his sights on Great Britain, Prime Minister Winston Churchill rallied his discouraged country: "Never give up. Never, never, never give up!"

They didn't. And neither should you. Jesus offers even greater encouragement: *"Ask, and it shall be given to you; seek, and you shall find; knock, and it shall be opened to you. For everyone who asks receives, and he who seeks finds, and to him who knocks it shall be opened"* (Matthew 7:7-8).

CHAPTER 3

Who Should Budget and Why

Many people are surprised to learn that approximately two-thirds of Jesus's parables are about money.

Keep in mind that Jesus never said money or material things were problems. He said they were symptoms of the real problem. Money itself is neither good nor bad, moral nor immoral. It is the *use* of money and your *perspective* that count.

Therefore, Jesus constantly warned us to guard our hearts against greed, ego, and pride. These are the tools Satan uses to control and manipulate this world—and us!

The apostle Paul wrote: *"Do not let immorality or any impurity or greed even be named among you, as is proper among saints. For this you know with certainty, that no immoral or impure person or covetous man, who is an idolater, has an inheritance in the kingdom of Christ and God"* (Ephesians 5:3,5).

In upcoming chapters we'll take a look at a simple budget plan you can use now, as well as after graduation. We'll also talk about credit cards, debit cards, and how to balance a checkbook. Each of these subjects is important, but none will make a profound difference in your finances until you come to grips with God's role in your finances.

Most folks have an upside-down view of money. They figure the money they have is theirs; *God's* money is just the portion they put in the collection basket. But God, who just happens to be the creator of all things, and the smartest one in the universe, has a different view.

As Lord and King, God owns *everything*—including the money we call our own. He has clear ideas of what He wants us to do with His money.

You are about to embark on the next leg of your journey into the future. It's time to learn what God has to say about money. Now more than ever, it's time to manage money according to God's plan.

I've come up with seven steps to help you do this. These are big steps. They require your best effort. But if you follow them, you will change your future.

Step 1: **Transfer Ownership**

God has placed the toughest step of all right at the front. Once you accomplish this step, all the others will fall into place. Here's why.

As a Christian, God expects us to transfer ownership of every possession to Him. This means money, time, parents, brothers, sisters, girlfriends, boyfriends, education, future career and earning power, and things like cars, clothes, and other possessions.

Did I leave anyone or anything out? If I did, go ahead and add that to your list. God expects it all. In fact, if you believe that you're the owner of even a single possession, then the events affecting that possession are going to affect your attitude.

The key is the proper understanding of stewardship. By Webster's definition, a steward is "one who manages another's property." We are, in reality, merely stewards of God's property while we're here on Earth. God will not force His will on us. If we make a total transfer of everything to God, He will keep His promise to provide every need we have through physical, material, and spiritual means—according to His perfect plan.

Sound simple? Trust me, it's not. Irrespective of age, we are all very accustomed to self-management of our belongings. Yet, there is absolutely no substitute for this first step. Once we transfer ownership of everything in our lives to God, it's at this point that we can experience financial freedom. It doesn't matter whether you're still in high school, a senior in college, or a soon-to-be bank president, financial freedom comes from knowing that God is in control.

Step 2: Stay Out of Debt

Although we'll take a closer look at debt in the next chapter, let me give you some tips that may help you as you map out your college strategy.

First, you need to have a *written plan* of all expenditures in their order of importance. Determine whether the expense or purchase is a need, a want, or a desire.

Needs are pretty obvious—things like food, clothing, and housing. "And if we have food and covering, with these we shall be content" (1 Timothy 6:8).

Wants can also appear awfully important. For example, you *need* clothes, but do you need the latest, most expensive style? That kind of outfit is a *want*. You *need* food, but do you need a steak and lobster dinner? That kind of meal is a *want*.

Desires are tougher. They don't exactly seem like needs, but they could be—if you rationalize them. Maybe the old car you have works fine, but if you got a *new* car, you wouldn't have to worry about it breaking down while you're taking all your non-Christian friends to church.

There's nothing wrong with desiring nice stuff. But if it rearranges your priorities, takes your attention from what's important, and gets you into debt, you're in trouble. After you work out your budget in the next chapter, you'll find that when all your financial obligations are out of the way, what's left is for whatever you want or desire.

Second, you need to open a *savings account* and get in the habit of putting something into savings every week or every month, regardless of how small the amount. The amount of your deposit is not nearly as important as making the deposit.

Establish a goal for your savings. Is it for tuition? A vacation?

A new car? Whatever the purpose, be consistent in your practice. *"There is precious treasure and oil in the dwelling of the wise, but a foolish man swallows it up"* (Proverbs 21:20).

Step 3: Establish the Tithe

Every Christian should establish the tithe as a minimum testimony to God's ownership. In every case, God wants you to give back to Him the first part of what He has given you. *"Honor the Lord from your wealth, and from the first of all your produce"* (Proverbs 3:9).

It's through sharing that you bring His power in finances into focus. If a sacrifice is necessary, do not sacrifice God's share. *"Now this I say, he who sows sparingly shall also reap sparingly; and he who sows bountifully shall also reap bountifully"* (2 Corinthians 9:6).

Step 4: Accept God's Provision

To get real financial peace, recognize and accept that God's *provision*—all that He gives you—is used to direct your life. *"My God shall supply all your needs according to His riches in glory in Christ Jesus"* (Philippians 4:19).

Many get the impression that God can direct us only by an abundance of money. Not true. Sometimes He directs us by withholding the abundance. We are called to live on what God provides and not be pressured by driving desires for wealth and material things.

Step 5: Put Others First

A Christian seeking financial freedom must always be willing to put other people first. *"Be hospitable to one another without complaint. As each one has received a special gift, employ it in serving one another, as good stewards of the manifold grace of God"* (1 Peter 4:9-10).

It does not mean that we are to be used as floor mats; but it does mean that we are not to profit at the loss or disadvantage of someone else.

Step 6: Avoid Indulgence

Unfortunately, most of us are self-indulgers, rarely passing up a want or desire, much less a need. To achieve financial freedom, you must avoid the indulgences of life. *"If anyone wishes to come after Me, let him deny himself, and take up his cross daily, and follow Me"* (Luke 9:23).

Step 7: Avoid Snap Decisions

Sooner or later someone will try to pressure you into making a quick financial decision through intimidation. *"The plans of the diligent lead surely to advantage, but everyone who is hasty come surely to poverty"* (Proverbs 21:5).

Unless you are on your guard, you may fall prey to a get-rich-quick scheme. Seek good counsel. Pray about the situation. Wait on God. *"Rest in the Lord and wait patiently for Him; do not fret because of him who prospers in his way, because of the man who carries out wicked schemes"* (Psalm 37:7).

These seven steps will help you begin to look at money from God's perspective. Now let's get down to dollars and cents. How do you manage this money carefully, to be sure it's being used the way God wants it to be? That's what you'll find out in the next chapter.

CHAPTER 4

Money Management 101

Do you think budgeting is boring? I used to think so. When I was in college, my idea of a budget was based totally on my checkbook. It was a very simple procedure: If I had blank checks left, I had money to spend. As ridiculous as that sounds, many people today still operate on that same assumption.

Actually, having complete control over your money is anything but boring. In fact, it can be fun. And it certainly is a lot better than the way I operated years ago. To help you get started, let me give you an easy formula:

$$AI - T\&T = NSI$$

If you can remember that, you'll never have a problem with handling money—now or in the future. It doesn't matter whether you have $125 a month coming in or you are earning $6,800 a month as an engineer. It all works the same.

Here's what it means:

AI stands for "Available Income." That's pretty self-explanatory, isn't it?

T&T in the formula means "Tithe and Taxes."

NSI means "Net Spendable Income." NSI is what you can *spend*.

See, it's simple: AI minus T&T equals NSI. You don't have to be a math student. Just plug it into your memory bank under "data, save."

If you're a student at Harvard and you are asked to present a financial plan for operating a multi-million dollar corporation and you propose the formula above, you probably will be ushered out of the class. Yet, if corporations, governments, and families alike adopted the plan, everyone could benefit.

Your Budget

On page 37 you'll find a Monthly Income and Expenses worksheet. Get a pencil; we're going to fill it out together right now to show you how it works. (There's another copy of it in the back of the book, which you can photocopy a bunch of times and use later.)

If you're not in college yet, this process will take some imagination on your part: You need to imagine what your life and finances will be like in college. And if you're already in college, or you've been living on your own for a while, this budget will help you immediately!

Remember, this is a worksheet. It's going to change as you learn more about your finances, but right now you can do a pretty good job of estimating the numbers for each line. If you're like most people, your income and expenses fluctuate from month to month. Later, I'll show you how to use separate "accounts" to allow for these monthly variations in income and expenses. For now, just add up a year's worth of each variable and divide it by 12 to get a monthly average.

Ready to start budgeting? Let's take it from the top!

AI: **Available Income.** For the purpose of establishing a budget, your AI includes any source of income: paychecks, investment income, parents, financial aid (scholarships, grants, loans), savings account, and birthday checks from your grandparents. In other words, list all money coming to you, from all sources, as income.

T&T: **Tithe & Taxes.** This budget doesn't break out your income for tax and tithe purposes. You'll need to work out the details on these two obligations separately. If you were to use your total AI to figure these obligations, you'd probably be paying twice for some things. For example, if you tithe on money when you earn it, then there's no need to tithe on it again when you withdraw it from your savings account. And if you're still a dependent and your parents pay taxes on the money they earn to help pay your college expenses, you (as a dependent) don't have to pay taxes on their contribution.

If you filed a tax return form for last year, you can use this form to estimate what your future taxes will be. If you've never filed a tax return before, the easiest way to estimate your taxes for budgeting is to fill out a "pretend" return. Your local library keeps copies of the tax booklets on file. You can photocopy the forms from one of these booklets and fill them out, using the details from your AI estimates and the numbers you come up with on the rest of your budget.

The tax form guides you through some simple addition and subtraction to come up with your *taxable* income. The tables in the booklet can show you the amount of tax you'd pay on that income.

Tithing is another matter. The amount of your tithe and who you tithe to are between you and God. Go down your list of income sources and decide which sources apply to your tithe. As I mentioned above, some of the dollars in your AI may have been tithed on already. Apply your percentage to the "tithable" income and you've got your tithe amount.

NSI: **Net Spendable Income.** Once you've listed all your sources of incoming money (AI) and subtracted your tithe and taxes (T&T), you have your NSI. To make your budget work, you must make sure that all your expenses can be covered with your NSI. This worksheet includes a list of common college expenses. Some of these items are always the same. These are called *fixed expenses:* rent, car payments, insurance.

The balance of your expenses are the most difficult to get a handle on because they vary from month to month and even from day to day: money for entertainment, books, clothes, and so on. Do your best at coming up with a year's worth of each expense item; then divide by 12 for your monthly figure.

Since everyone has different ideas about what expenses are, I've given you specific categories to plug your numbers into. If the categories don't apply to you, leave them blank. But for the areas that do affect your overall budget, be as accurate as you can. If you need help to come up with realistic amounts, ask other college students or your parents. Some college financial aid offices have budgeting tips and information that can help you estimate the costs of living on or off campus.

Monthly Income & Expenses

AVAILABLE INCOME (AI)
Wages and Tips _____
From Savings _____
Financial Aid (loans, grants, scholarships) _____
Parents _____
Other _____
TOTAL AI _____

TITHE & TAXES (T&T)
Tithe _____
Taxes (including taxes withheld) _____
TOTAL T&T _____
NET SPENDABLE INCOME (NSI): AI minus T&T _____

EXPENSES

HOUSING
Rent _____
Utilities _____
Telephone _____
Furniture & Appliances _____

FOOD
Meal Plan _____
Groceries _____

TRANSPORTATION
Car Payment _____
Car Insurance _____
Gas & Oil _____
Car Repairs _____
Public Transit _____
Other _____

EDUCATION
Tuition & Fees
Lab Fees _____
Other Fees _____
Books _____

MEDICAL
Doctor
Dentist _____
Prescriptions _____
Other _____

OTHER LIVING EXPENSES
Clothing
Laundry _____
Household Supplies _____
Personal Care (toiletries, hair care) _____
Entertainment (dining, movies, events) _____
Gifts
Monthly Dues _____
Misc. Expenses _____

FINANCIAL
Savings Deposits
Other Investments _____
Insurance (other than car) _____
Debt & Loan Repayments (other than car) _____
Credit Card payment
Loans _____
Other _____

TOTAL EXPENSES _____

This Is Fun?

You're probably questioning my comment that money management can be fun. Before you write me off, hear me out. Not only can you always know just how much money you have available (you'll be the envy of everyone on campus), but you'll also be challenged each month to see if you can make the numbers work for you—and still have some money left over to spend on something you just can't live without.

Keep in mind that the numbers you plug in are *your* numbers. No one is telling you just how much you should allocate for each category. Although I can suggest some estimates, the final decision is up to you. Obviously, if you allocate 78 percent of all your NSI on food, you won't have much left to distribute to the other areas, such as rent, books, car payments, and clothes.

But here's the best part. The figures are also flexible. For example, if you allocate $10 each month for medical and after six or seven months you're still alive and well, why not move some of those dollars over to another category that may be running short each month—you know, money for dates, movies, fun stuff. The more flexible your plan, the more flexible you can be.

Accounting 101

Now that you have a budget, you need to manage it properly to make it work for you. The easiest way to manage your budget is to set up "accounts" for each of your categories. I'll show you how in a moment. But first, let me tell you why.

Let's say that your tuition for one year is $12,000. Your monthly budget for that expense shows $1,000. But you don't get to *pay* the tuition in 12 small chunks. It's due in two big chunks—$6,000 at the start of each term. To make these big payments, you must set aside $1,000 in each of the six months preceding the next term.

Other expenses vary from month to month. For example, if you live at school during the school year and move back home for the summer, your housing expenses drop during the summer. Separate accounts for each of these expense categories can prevent you from spending money one month that will be needed the next.

Pretend for a moment that you have a separate checking account for each of your categories. In the above example, you'd deposit $1,000 in your tuition checking account for six straight months; then write a $6,000 check at the start of the term, and repeat this process for the next term. In the housing account, your balance would grow during the summer and shrink during the school year. Of course, it's impractical to open a checking account for each of your categories. But you *can* keep separate ledgers on each category.

Instead of depositing money into separate bank accounts, you can keep individual category ledgers and deposit all the money in one checking account. When you deposit your paycheck, all the money goes into your checking account. But portions of that money are divided among your various expense categories and recorded in their ledgers. Likewise, when you write a check, the money comes out of your checking account, but you also record the withdrawal in the appropriate category ledger.

With separate ledger pages, keeping to your budget is simple. Can you afford to buy concert tickets? Don't look in your checking account—that money's already accounted for. Look at your entertainment category ledger: It will show you how much of the money in your checking account has been set aside for entertainment.

We've included a blank Individual Category Ledger in the back of the book. Make copies for each of your expense categories and record each "transaction" on the appropriate ledger.

Pretty soon you will have mastered your budget and won't even have to think about it. Yet, it will be there working for you, putting you in control of your finances instead of the other way around. I like that. And you will too!

What About Debt?

Debt is the one thing that can kill a budget quicker than anything else. Debt is a destroyer. It has ruined many marriages, caused broken homes, and can wreck your college years, and beyond, if it's not under control.

Debt comes in various shapes and styles. And like many things, before the debt comes pleasure. Who would think that using a credit card for gasoline, or clothes, or a nice restaurant could possibly come back to haunt you? It often does. I'll talk more about credit cards later.

What about other debts like school loans, car payments, and installment payments for furniture or appliances? How can you survive the monthly burden of paying for things you bought in the past? People with the greatest of intentions often are led down the debt path before they even realize it. And while they may be very serious about their purchases, oftentimes they are seriously wrong.

Remember that half of all marriages in America fail, and 80 percent of those that fail were having financial problems. Solomon said, *"The rich rules over the poor, and the borrower becomes the lender's slave"* (Proverbs 22:7). Right now, however, you have the advantage! Once you master "Money Management 101" you will never be a slave to debt or the debt peddlers (finance companies).

After you enter the numbers in your budget each month, you'll know exactly how much you can spend when the impulse to buy hits you. The impulse is not wrong. We all have impulses—sometimes daily. It's when we give in to impulse buying that we set ourselves up for potential financial disaster.

Car Loans

Car payments are a big budget buster among college students. Used car lots are filled with almost-new cars whose young owners couldn't survive the first year of payments. When you miss a couple of loan payments, the lender repossesses your car, and your down payment and any monthly payments you made are lost forever.

You lose all that money because your shiny new car typically drops 30 to 40 percent in value the moment you drive it off the lot. It can take years of monthly payments before you can sell that car for more than the amount you still owe on the loan.

Even if you can manage the car payments, the price of a new car may cost you in other areas. For example, you can spend all summer working to pay for your fancy new German car; or you can buy a good used car and use the money you save to pay for a trip to Germany. Big car payments translate into more time at work and less time and money for other things.

That's why I usually recommend buying a used car. Let someone else pay the premium for that new-car smell. Of course, buying a used car is risky too: you know little about the car except what the seller tells you—and he or she may not be trustworthy. If you're able to find the little old lady (not necessarily from Pasadena) who likes to purchase a new car every year yet rarely takes that car out of the garage, make a fast trip to her house and buy her barely used vehicle.

Failing that, you'll need to do some work to get a good deal. First, do some homework: Go to the library and look through the consumer information on used cars. There you'll find guides listing every car make, model, year, and the results of surveys taken by their owners. These surveys help you identify cars that are reliable and inexpensive to maintain. This is important: An unreliable car can cost you as much in big repair bills as the payments on a new car.

After you've done your homework and identified reliable car models, it's time to do some legwork. Read the auto ads and find cars that match your model list and price range. Then check out several of these cars in person. You'll start to develop an idea of what kind of car you can expect for the price: its physical condition, the number of miles on the odometer, and the like.

Finally, when you've found a car that's right for you, take along someone who's good at auto work. Your mechanic friend may be able to spot hidden damage or potential problems that you might miss—and the seller isn't telling you. Sure, this kind of car shopping takes more time. But remember: Every dollar you save in price now—and don't spend on future repairs later—translates into less time at work, or more money for other priorities. It's worth the effort.

Buying on Credit

Each year Christian Financial Concepts counsels thousands of American families in financial trouble. For most of these families, credit purchasing is the main reason for their financial bondage. Our federal government is suffering from the same debilitating restraints.

Our society breeds on credit and credit cards; consumer accounts are everywhere and available to virtually anyone—including college students. Credit cards and store accounts are tempting pseudo-solutions to the problem of wanting something but not having the money to buy it. But before you sign on the dotted line for 12, 24, or 36 months, go back to your budget and work on a plan that will enable you to purchase those items with cash—after just a few months of careful budget manipulation. With a decent budget and a little patience, you'll find that you can avoid borrowing to buy the things you need.

The federal government has made it easy for college students to borrow money regardless of parent income. Some students think that borrowing is the easiest way—or only way—to finance their education. Think again. The cost to your future is great—especially when you discover that you could have done it a better way. Before you sign away your future to pay for your present education, look back at the alternative funding ideas in Chapter 2. Make "no debt" a goal; you'll be surprised at how far you can go.

Remember when I said you'd be the envy of everyone on campus when you knew exactly how much money you always had available? The same thing is true after you get out of school. Pity the poor graduate who never had a budget and now is making an outstanding income, only to be totally bogged down with payments: car, house, furniture, student loan, insurance, department store, and credit card—you get the picture. *Now* is the time to paint a different picture for yourself.

When you exercise the simple formula, AI less T&T equals NSI, you take control of your finances, rather than having the finances take control of you!

CHAPTER 5

Checkbook Management

Reconciliation is a big word and it means big things. For example, if you have a falling out with one of your college professors, you might want to reconcile that before grades come out. In this case, it simply means to fix a strained or disharmonious relationship.

It's also a word used for balancing a checkbook. And there is nothing more disharmonious than having a balance in your checkbook that doesn't agree with anyone or anything. If you haven't yet experienced that trial, consider yourself among the fortunate few. It truly is a balancing act.

Recently I heard of a 27-year-old man who is about to graduate from medical school. To finance his lifelong dream of becoming a doctor, he borrowed heavily from one of the lending institutions that was eager to loan young would-be doctors tons of money. As he nears graduation and the start of a three-year residency training program, he not only owes $60,000 in student loans, but he has little idea of how to balance a checkbook.

Without a basic course in budgeting and bank reconciliation, he may well succeed in the more complex operating procedures but fail in one of life's simpler operations. How simple? Keep reading.

Your Record

Numbers are among the hardest things to remember. And since a checkbook is all about numbers, recording these numbers is critical to your checkbook success. That's what the register is for. It's the form in the front of your checkbook where you record all transactions. The first step to checking account management is to record each transaction in your register.

One of the best ways to keep your records straight is to buy duplicate checks. Each time you write a check, your pen makes a carbonless copy of it on a duplicate check immediately beneath it. This duplicate gives you an automatic record of the transaction: who the check was written to, the amount, what it was for, and when it was written. If you forget to record the transaction in your checkbook register, you can go back to the duplicate to get all the information you need.

Likewise, each time you go to the Automatic Teller Machine (ATM) and request cash on the spot, save the ATM receipt. And whenever you make a deposit save the receipt. Then use these receipts to record the transactions in your register.

The Bank's Record

Of course, you're not the only one keeping a record of your checking account transactions. The bank is keeping its own version and each month it sends you a copy of that record, called a *statement*. The bank statement lists your transactions for the past month: deposits, ATM withdrawals, checks cashed, service fees, and so on.

In a perfect world, your record (the check register) and their record (the statement) would be identical, and there would be no need to balance your checking account. But for all sorts of reasons, the two records often disagree. For example, you record checks as they're written, and the bank records checks as they're *cashed*. So if you write a check to someone who buries it somewhere and forgets about it, the bank's record will show more money than yours—until your absentminded friend finds the check and cashes it. And if you write a check at the end of the month and the check gets cashed at the beginning of the next month, the records will disagree for a while.

Reconciliation

The process of getting these two records to agree is called reconciliation. It's a big word, but it's easier than it sounds. Simply follow these five steps:

Step 1: Compare Checks. Determine which checks have been cashed. Do this by placing a mark in the checkbook register next to each check number that's listed on the statement. Mark these check numbers in the statement too.

Step 2: Compare Deposits and Withdrawals. Do the same thing with deposits and withdrawals, marking each transaction that's listed on both your register and the bank statement. Remember to mark them in both places.

Step 3: Record Their Surprises. Look on their statement for unmarked transactions. If you find one, it means that you don't have a record of that transaction in your register. Maybe you forgot to record a check or an ATM withdrawal or you were charged a service fee because your balance fell below a certain level. Record each of these surprises into your register and mark them off in both places as you do. If your new balance matches theirs, you're reconciled! If not, go to the next step.

Step 4: Add Your New Credits. All transactions are now in your register, but you may have a few transactions that didn't make it into the bank's record before the statement was printed. First of all, look through your register for unmarked deposits. If you find any without a mark, write down the amount of these "credits" on the back of the bank statement. Add the total of these credits to the bank's version of your balance.

Step 5: Subtract Your New Debits. You may also have some checks or ATM withdrawals that didn't get cashed or recorded in time to make it onto the bank statement. These "debits" are the ones listed in your register that don't have marks next to them. Write down these debit amounts on the back of the bank statement and subtract them from the amount you got in step four. Now you've adjusted the bank's version to include all the transactions they didn't know about when they printed the statement. Does this new number match the balance in your register? You're reconciled!

What happens if you do all five steps and your number is still different than theirs? Someone made a mistake. Review the steps and make sure all transactions were recorded and marked properly. Then go over your arithmetic to be sure you didn't slip a digit somewhere. If you're sure that your numbers are right, then the error may be theirs. They make mistakes too, and you may spot one while you're checking the figures. Go into the bank and show your statement and your register. The bank will fix the error.

One More Reconciliation

Some students who have mastered the art of reconciling a checkbook still suffer from financial problems. That's because they've reconciled their record with the bank's record, *but they haven't reconciled their spending with their budget.*

A balanced checkbook is key to successful money management. But the checks you write must fit within your budget. If you buy a new stereo with a check that doesn't bounce, that's a good thing. But if that money was meant to buy books for school, what good is a balanced checkbook?

Remember that your checking account isn't a thing on its own—it's an extension of your budget. The checks you write and the deposits and withdrawals you make must fit within your budget. Remember that your budget is the blueprint to successful money management. Your checking account is an important tool you'll use to carry out that plan.

Note of Interest

Some banks now offer a bank debit card, which looks like a Visa or MasterCard but works like a check. Here's the difference: A credit card transaction is a loan. When you charge something, you're borrowing someone else's money to pay for it. If you don't pay back the lender right away, you pay interest. When you pay for something with a debit card, you're spending your own money—straight out of your bank account. Think of it as an electronic check. But there's a key difference.

Paper checks often have a "float" period. After you write them, they may float in the system for a day or two before the bank takes the money out of your account. There's no "float" period with a debit card transaction. The moment you make the transaction, the money is withdrawn from your account. So don't try to use a debit card one day and then race to the bank the next morning with a deposit to cover it: you'll be overdrawn before you get there.

Like all checking account transactions, it's important to record every debit card use in your register.

CHAPTER 6

Credit Card Management

Are credit cards a curse or a blessing? They can be either, depending on how you use them. Let's take a look at how credit cards work, and then I'll show you how to use them as a blessing and avoid their many curses.

Technically speaking, the credit card is an incredible advancement in the world of finances. You can be in a store in Amsterdam or Prague, St. Louis or Seattle, and if you have a credit card you don't need cash. Just hand over the card, sign your name, and collect your merchandise.

Thirty or forty days later, you'll receive a printed statement itemizing your shopping spree. All you have to do is pay the bill. What could be easier?

It truly is simple and very convenient if (and that's a big IF) you pay the full amount on the statement as soon as it's received.

The problem begins with a tiny line on the statement: *Minimum Payment Due.* The number after those intoxicating words is awfully attractive—and a lot smaller than the number showing your total balance. In fact, I believe it is one of the most deliciously destructive traps ever devised. Once it catches you, it doesn't let go.

Interest Free—*for Some*

When addressing college students on the subject of credit, author and speaker Gerri Detweiler described the "minimum payment syndrome" as a clever means contrived by the banks to make lots of money. Even though the banks want you to believe that they're the good guys on white horses, nothing could be further from the truth. When you opt to pay a little at a time, you automatically lose the "grace period," and you pay the maximum interest rate.

The grace period is the difference between the date you first make a purchase and the date your payment is due. If you pay the full amount within that period, there is a grace period, or free ride, with no interest charge—usually 25 or 30 days after the statement is printed. That's a good thing. Now for the bad news.

This wonderful grace period applies only if you paid off last month's balance in full. If you had an unpaid balance from last month (i.e., you still owe money on the card), you're charged interest on any new purchases from the moment you make them. No grace period. No free ride. And for many, there's no way out.

If you pay the minimum payment amount, or any amount less than the full balance owed, you're charged interest on *everything*—old purchases, new purchases—and that interest is added *daily*.

In her book *The Ultimate Credit Handbook* (Plume 1993) Detweiler says, "A credit card is nothing more than a means of accessing a personal loan but, because of the glitzy advertising, few people think of a card that way. Instead, we think of credit cards as a means of convenience, a shortcut to the 'good life,' symbols of financial success, or even an extension of our income."

Detweiler offers some pretty healthy advice for college students, as well as those in the workplace. "If you have a balance of $1,000 at 19.8 percent interest (typical) with a card that has an annual fee of $20, and you choose to pay a minimum of 3 percent of the unpaid balance each month, it will take a total of 8 years to pay off the debt, cost $843 in finance charges and another $180 in card membership fees."

The bottom line: That good deal you picked up for only a $1,000 will really cost you over $2,000 when paid in full. Welcome to the real world.

As I pointed out before, credit cards themselves are not the problem. It's all in how you use them. If you use your credit card only to pay for things in your budget *and* you pay the balance in full every month, there's no problem. Do this, and you've got a convenient way to pay for things and a growing, stellar credit record to help you in the future. That's a blessing.

If You're a Student, You're a Target!

I know a college student who obtained 28 credit cards, which he frequently and proudly displayed to his female friends as a measure of his success. Although he was only 18 when he started his collection, he had the same name as his father, and he used that to his advantage—or in this case, to his disadvantage. Before long he began to use one card to pay off another card, and by the time he reached his 20th birthday, this young college student had accumulated nearly $10,000 in debt!

College students are attractive targets for lending institutions. Even without any established credit, lenders are eager to capture your loyalty—and your wallet. In fact, banks spend millions of dollars each year luring unwary students with special campus promotions, no-annual-fee cards, gold cards, frequent flyer miles, special discounts on new cars, and other incentives.

Detweiler writes that CitiBank is the leader in issuing cards to college students. "Their applications litter the dormitories and classrooms of every campus in America. . .and they're easy to get. But beware, most of the major credit cards offered through college programs are not cheap. The cards usually carry high interest rates."

Shopping for a Card

The deluge of credit card offers can work to your advantage. With many card issuers competing for your business, you can afford to shop around and choose a card that's best. Visa and

MasterCard don't issue credit cards. They're kind of like franchises, in that banks and other institutions offer these "name brand" cards themselves—and each issuer is free to set the terms of the card as it wishes. And these terms vary greatly from one issuer to the next.

Here's how to find the best deal: First of all, look for a card that comes with no or a low annual fee. Second, take a good look at the grace period—they vary from bank to bank. Some issuers give 25 or 30 days, some give you a shorter free ride. A few issuers give you NO grace period. Your reply to such offers is simple: "No grace? No! Period."

Third, look at the interest rate. If after all you've just read, you somehow manage to miss paying a balance in full and get stuck with interest, it helps to have that interest as low as possible. But remember that even the lowest interest rate offered on credit cards is *exorbitant*. Do anything you can to avoid paying interest.

Next, look for other benefits. If the card offers airline mileage and you're going to school far from home, wise use of the card may get you a free flight home for Christmas. But beware; many issuers throw all sorts of "benefits" and services at you that you either don't need or can find cheaper elsewhere. For example, "deals" on merchandise offered with the card are usually no bargain; you can find a better selection at a lower price on your own.

Finally, pay attention to the fine print. Card issuers are notorious for tacking on charges that will wipe out your budget: late payment fees, fees for charging over your credit limit, bounced checks, and so on. Compare these charges among issuers, and in all cases avoid doing anything that will get one of these charges slapped onto your account.

With so many credit card offers out there, it seems that anyone can get one. But it's possible that you may be turned down. Some students who have trouble getting credit may be tempted to have someone cosign for them. Cosigning is risky business.

Anyone who cosigns for a loan is signing a legal contract and will be held responsible for the entire debt. The Lord puts it this way: *"Do not be among those who give pledges, among those who become sureties for debts"* (Proverbs 22:26). In other words, don't ask anyone to cosign for you, and do not become a guarantor (cosigner) for someone else.

If you need a credit card but have been turned down, establish credit the old-fashioned way: Apply for a gasoline or department store card, whose issuers are eager for your business. Make a necessary, budgeted purchase each month and pay the balance in full. The issuer will send a record of your spotless payment habits to credit reporting agencies. In a year, you'll have a small but sparkling credit record, which can be seen by anyone considering you for a bigger credit card.

If you still get turned down for a bigger card and you have no history of bad credit, there may be a mistake on your credit record. Request a copy from the credit reporting agency (look under "Credit" in the phone book and call to find out how to do this). You may discover that credit information belonging to someone with your same name, or a relative with a similar name, has ended up on your credit record. If that person has bad credit, you're paying the price until you straighten things out with the credit reporting agency.

Taming a Wild Card
If you get into deep debt with plastic, the card isn't the one that needs to be tamed; it's you and your buying habits. If your balance gets out of hand, act immediately to get it back into line. There are some taming tricks.

1. Stop Now. If you let a balance roll-over into the next month, *stop there*! Do not use your card again (any new purchase gets hit with interest the moment you make it), and pay off the old balance in full immediately so it doesn't continue to accrue interest. (It's surprising how many people forget that the way out of a hole is *up*, not down.)

2. Pay Now. The dreaded interest is stacking up daily, so don't wait until your next statement to make a payment. As soon as you have the money, send a check with your card account number on it to the issuer; the interest madness stops the day after they get your check. If you can't pay it off with one check, send them another one the following week. Do this until the account is back to zero. (Don't know what your balance is? Call. That's what the 800 number is for.)

3. Flee from Fees. See to it that your payments arrive before the deadline. If you miss it, you'll be hit with a fat late fee *and* interest on the account balance. If you know you're going to be late, call the issuer and tell them. Sometimes they'll cut you some slack—but only if they hear from you. (With creditors, absences makes their heart grow *harder.*) If the check bounces, you're slammed with another fee. And if you go over your credit limit, you may be hit with still another penalty.

4. Toss the Offers. When you open your statement and all those offers for insurance and merchandise fall out, dump them in the trash. You don't need what they're selling—and if you do, you'll find it cheaper elsewhere. (Hint: Dorm rooms are small enough already; don't make it smaller by filling it with junk.)

5. Cancel. When all else fails, destroy the card. When it comes down to a battle of who's controlling whom, concede the battle and cut up the card. A wild credit card habit is a sign that your budget and money management skills aren't perfected. Take a time-out from the credit game and work on the basics. You'll thank yourself later and get another card when you're ready.

I know what you're thinking. A few dollars in fees and interest isn't going to kill you. You're right. . .right now. But the card habits you establish now will be with you for the rest of your life. Get it right, right from the start, and you'll be all right later on. But if you mess up now, you'll be fighting your bad habits (and your bad credit record) for years to come. I've seen the sad result of these habits in thousands of lives and I know that *now* is the best time for you to prevent financial disaster in your future.

So there you have it. A wisely managed credit card can be a real help to your money management and financial future. Or it can be a debt-trap that ensnares you now and holds you captive for years to come. Blessing or curse: The choice is yours!

CHAPTER 7

Epilogue

Years ago, when I first began financial counseling, nearly everyone had some kind of debt problem, and in virtually every case it had been around for a long time. Quite often these people had first gotten into debt while in college and had not lived a day debt-free since then, even though in many cases their households had two sizeable incomes.

If these people had applied the biblical principles of money management addressed in this book, they would be far better off than those who failed to develop a budget until they were nearly forced into bankruptcy.

At Christian Financial Concepts we receive thousands of letters and phone calls each year from people asking for help in financial management. In every case we respond with the same message: Develop a workable budget.

If you will establish even the simplest of all budgets, like the one found in chapter 4, you will never have to face the pressure, the trauma, and the embarrassment of facing debt collectors.

Incidentally, it's not just low- and middle-income people who face financial crises. Recently I heard of a well-meaning doctor who was considering filing bankruptcy, simply because he was so far behind on his student loan payments.

As I mentioned earlier, developing and living on a budget can be very rewarding. The freedom that comes to those who follow a budget is the kind of freedom God intended for all of us to have.

If you follow the seven steps to financial freedom found in chapter 3, the term "financial bondage" will never be part of your vocabulary, and your college years will be the beginning of a lifetime of good spending and saving habits.

Christian Financial Concepts Inc.

Teaching | Biblical Principles of Managing Money

Larry Burkett, founder and president of Christian Financial Concepts, is the best-selling author of more than 50 books on business and personal finances. He also hosts two of CFC's four radio programs broadcast on hundreds of stations worldwide.

Larry earned B.S. degrees in marketing and finance, and recently an Honorary Doctorate in Economics was conferred by Southwest Baptist University. For several years Larry served as a manager in the space program at Cape Canaveral, Florida. He also has been vice president of an electronics manufacturing firm. Larry's education, business experience, and solid understanding of God's Word enable him to give practical, Bible-based financial counsel to families, churches, and businesses.

Founded in 1976, Christian Financial Concepts is a nonprofit, nondenominational ministry dedicated to helping God's people gain a clear understanding of how to manage their money according to scriptural principles. Although practical assistance is provided on many levels, the purpose of CFC is simply *to bring glory to God by freeing His people from financial bondage so they may serve Him to their utmost.*

One major avenue of ministry involves the training of volunteers in budget and debt counseling and linking them with financially troubled families and individuals through a nationwide referral network. CFC also provides financial management seminars and workshops for churches and other groups. (Formats available include audio, video, and live instruction.) A full line of printed and audio-visual materials related to money management is available through CFC's materials department (1-800-722-1976) or via the Internet (http://www.cfcministry.org).

Life Pathways, another outreach of Christian Financial Concepts, helps teenagers and adults find their occupational calling. The Life Pathways *Career Direct* assessment package gauges a person's work priorities, skills, vocational interests, and personality. Reports in each of these areas define a person's strengths, weaknesses, and unique, God-given pattern for work.

Visit CFC's Internet site at http://www.cfcministry.org or write to the address below for further information.

Christian Financial Concepts
PO Box 2377
Gainesville, GA 30503

MONTHLY INCOME & EXPENSES WORKSHEET

AVAILABLE INCOME (AI)

Wages and Tips _____

From Savings _____

Financial Aid (loans, grants, scholarships) _____

Parents _____

Other _____

TOTAL AI _____

TITHE & TAXES (T&T)

Tithe _____

Taxes (including taxes withheld) _____

TOTAL T&T _____

NET SPENDABLE INCOME (NSI) _____

EXPENSES

HOUSING

Rent _____

Utilities _____

Telephone _____

Furniture & Appliances _____

Other _____

FOOD

Meal Plan _____

Groceries _____

TRANSPORTATION

Car Payment _____

Car Insurance _____

Gas & Oil _____

Car Repairs _____

Public Transit _____

Other _____

EDUCATION

Tuition & Fees _____

Lab Fees _____

Other Fees _____

Books _____

MEDICAL

Doctor _____

Dentist _____

Prescriptions _____

Other _____

OTHER LIVING EXPENSES

Clothing _____

Laundry _____

Household Supplies _____

Personal Care (toiletries, hair cut/care) _____

Entertainment (dining, movies, events) _____

Gifts _____

Monthly Dues _____

Misc. Expenses _____

FINANCIAL

Savings Deposits _____

Other Investments _____

Insurance (other than car) _____

Debt & Loan Repayments (other than car) _____

Credit Card payment _____

Loans _____

Other _____

TOTAL EXPENSES _____

MONTHLY INCOME & EXPENSES WORKSHEET

AVAILABLE INCOME (AI)

Wages and Tips _____

From Savings _____

Financial Aid (loans, grants, scholarships) _____

Parents _____

Other _____

TOTAL AI _____

TITHE & TAXES (T&T)

Tithe _____

Taxes (including taxes withheld) _____

TOTAL T&T _____

NET SPENDABLE INCOME (NSI) _____

EXPENSES

HOUSING

Rent _____

Utilities _____

Telephone _____

Furniture & Appliances _____

Other _____

FOOD

Meal Plan _____

Groceries _____

TRANSPORTATION

Car Payment _____

Car Insurance _____

Gas & Oil _____

Car Repairs _____

Public Transit _____

Other _____

EDUCATION

Tuition & Fees _____

Lab Fees _____

Other Fees _____

Books _____

MEDICAL

Doctor _____

Dentist _____

Prescriptions _____

Other _____

OTHER LIVING EXPENSES

Clothing _____

Laundry _____

Household Supplies _____

Personal Care (toiletries, hair cut/care) _____

Entertainment (dining, movies, events) _____

Gifts _____

Monthly Dues _____

Misc. Expenses _____

FINANCIAL

Savings Deposits _____

Other Investments _____

Insurance (other than car) _____

Debt & Loan Repayments (other than car) _____

Credit Card payment _____

Loans _____

Other _____

TOTAL EXPENSES _____

MONTHLY INCOME & EXPENSES WORKSHEET

AVAILABLE INCOME (AI)

Wages and Tips _____

From Savings _____

Financial Aid (loans, grants, scholarships) _____

Parents _____

Other _____

TOTAL AI _____

TITHE & TAXES (T&T)

Tithe _____

Taxes (including taxes withheld) _____

TOTAL T&T _____

NET SPENDABLE INCOME (NSI) _____

EXPENSES

HOUSING

Rent _____

Utilities _____

Telephone _____

Furniture & Appliances _____

Other _____

FOOD

Meal Plan _____

Groceries _____

TRANSPORTATION

Car Payment _____

Car Insurance _____

Gas & Oil _____

Car Repairs _____

Public Transit _____

Other _____

EDUCATION

Tuition & Fees _____

Lab Fees _____

Other Fees _____

Books _____

MEDICAL

Doctor _____

Dentist _____

Prescriptions _____

Other _____

OTHER LIVING EXPENSES

Clothing _____

Laundry _____

Household Supplies _____

Personal Care (toiletries, hair cut/care) _____

Entertainment (dining, movies, events) _____

Gifts _____

Monthly Dues _____

Misc. Expenses _____

FINANCIAL

Savings Deposits _____

Other Investments _____

Insurance (other than car) _____

Debt & Loan Repayments (other than car) _____

Credit Card payment _____

Loans _____

Other _____

TOTAL EXPENSES _____

MONTHLY INCOME & EXPENSES WORKSHEET

AVAILABLE INCOME (AI)

Wages and Tips _____

From Savings _____

Financial Aid (loans, grants, scholarships) _____

Parents _____

Other _____

TOTAL AI _____

TITHE & TAXES (T&T)

Tithe _____

Taxes (including taxes withheld) _____

TOTAL T&T _____

NET SPENDABLE INCOME (NSI) _____

EXPENSES

HOUSING

Rent _____

Utilities _____

Telephone _____

Furniture & Appliances _____

Other _____

FOOD

Meal Plan _____

Groceries _____

TRANSPORTATION

Car Payment _____

Car Insurance _____

Gas & Oil _____

Car Repairs _____

Public Transit _____

Other _____

EDUCATION

Tuition & Fees _____

Lab Fees _____

Other Fees _____

Books _____

MEDICAL

Doctor _____

Dentist _____

Prescriptions _____

Other _____

OTHER LIVING EXPENSES

Clothing _____

Laundry _____

Household Supplies _____

Personal Care (toiletries, hair cut/care) _____

Entertainment (dining, movies, events) _____

Gifts _____

Monthly Dues _____

Misc. Expenses _____

FINANCIAL

Savings Deposits _____

Other Investments _____

Insurance (other than car) _____

Debt & Loan Repayments (other than car) _____

Credit Card payment _____

Loans _____

Other _____

TOTAL EXPENSES _____

MONTHLY INCOME & EXPENSES WORKSHEET

AVAILABLE INCOME (AI)

Wages and Tips _____

From Savings _____

Financial Aid (loans, grants, scholarships) _____

Parents _____

Other _____

TOTAL AI _____

TITHE & TAXES (T&T)

Tithe _____

Taxes (including taxes withheld) _____

TOTAL T&T _____

NET SPENDABLE INCOME (NSI) _____

EXPENSES

HOUSING

Rent _____

Utilities _____

Telephone _____

Furniture & Appliances _____

Other _____

FOOD

Meal Plan _____

Groceries _____

TRANSPORTATION

Car Payment _____

Car Insurance _____

Gas & Oil _____

Car Repairs _____

Public Transit _____

Other _____

EDUCATION

Tuition & Fees _____

Lab Fees _____

Other Fees _____

Books _____

MEDICAL

Doctor _____

Dentist _____

Prescriptions _____

Other _____

OTHER LIVING EXPENSES

Clothing _____

Laundry _____

Household Supplies _____

Personal Care (toiletries, hair cut/care) _____

Entertainment (dining, movies, events) _____

Gifts _____

Monthly Dues _____

Misc. Expenses _____

FINANCIAL

Savings Deposits _____

Other Investments _____

Insurance (other than car) _____

Debt & Loan Repayments (other than car) _____

Credit Card payment _____

Loans _____

Other _____

TOTAL EXPENSES _____

MONTHLY INCOME & EXPENSES WORKSHEET

AVAILABLE INCOME (AI)

Wages and Tips _____

From Savings _____

Financial Aid (loans, grants, scholarships) _____

Parents _____

Other _____

TOTAL AI _____

TITHE & TAXES (T&T)

Tithe _____

Taxes (including taxes withheld) _____

TOTAL T&T _____

NET SPENDABLE INCOME (NSI) _____

EXPENSES

HOUSING

Rent _____

Utilities _____

Telephone _____

Furniture & Appliances _____

Other _____

FOOD

Meal Plan _____

Groceries _____

TRANSPORTATION

Car Payment _____

Car Insurance _____

Gas & Oil _____

Car Repairs _____

Public Transit _____

Other _____

EDUCATION

Tuition & Fees _____

Lab Fees _____

Other Fees _____

Books _____

MEDICAL

Doctor _____

Dentist _____

Prescriptions _____

Other _____

OTHER LIVING EXPENSES

Clothing _____

Laundry _____

Household Supplies _____

Personal Care (toiletries, hair cut/care) _____

Entertainment (dining, movies, events) _____

Gifts _____

Monthly Dues _____

Misc. Expenses _____

FINANCIAL

Savings Deposits _____

Other Investments _____

Insurance (other than car) _____

Debt & Loan Repayments (other than car) _____

Credit Card payment _____

Loans _____

Other _____

TOTAL EXPENSES _____

MONTHLY INCOME & EXPENSES WORKSHEET

AVAILABLE INCOME (AI)

Wages and Tips _____

From Savings _____

Financial Aid (loans, grants, scholarships) _____

Parents _____

Other _____

TOTAL AI _____

TITHE & TAXES (T&T)

Tithe _____

Taxes (including taxes withheld) _____

TOTAL T&T _____

NET SPENDABLE INCOME (NSI) _____

EXPENSES

HOUSING

Rent _____

Utilities _____

Telephone _____

Furniture & Appliances _____

Other _____

FOOD

Meal Plan _____

Groceries _____

TRANSPORTATION

Car Payment _____

Car Insurance _____

Gas & Oil _____

Car Repairs _____

Public Transit _____

Other _____

EDUCATION

Tuition & Fees _____

Lab Fees _____

Other Fees _____

Books _____

MEDICAL

Doctor _____

Dentist _____

Prescriptions _____

Other _____

OTHER LIVING EXPENSES

Clothing _____

Laundry _____

Household Supplies _____

Personal Care (toiletries, hair cut/care) _____

Entertainment (dining, movies, events) _____

Gifts _____

Monthly Dues _____

Misc. Expenses _____

FINANCIAL

Savings Deposits _____

Other Investments _____

Insurance (other than car) _____

Debt & Loan Repayments (other than car) _____

Credit Card payment _____

Loans _____

Other _____

TOTAL EXPENSES _____

MONTHLY INCOME & EXPENSES WORKSHEET

AVAILABLE INCOME (AI)

Wages and Tips _____

From Savings _____

Financial Aid (loans, grants, scholarships) _____

Parents _____

Other _____

TOTAL AI _____

TITHE & TAXES (T&T)

Tithe _____

Taxes (including taxes withheld) _____

TOTAL T&T _____

NET SPENDABLE INCOME (NSI) _____

EXPENSES
HOUSING

Rent _____

Utilities _____

Telephone _____

Furniture & Appliances _____

Other _____

FOOD

Meal Plan _____

Groceries _____

TRANSPORTATION

Car Payment _____

Car Insurance _____

Gas & Oil _____

Car Repairs _____

Public Transit _____

Other _____

EDUCATION

Tuition & Fees _____

Lab Fees _____

Other Fees _____

Books _____

MEDICAL

Doctor _____

Dentist _____

Prescriptions _____

Other _____

OTHER LIVING EXPENSES

Clothing _____

Laundry _____

Household Supplies _____

Personal Care (toiletries, hair cut/care) _____

Entertainment (dining, movies, events) _____

Gifts _____

Monthly Dues _____

Misc. Expenses _____

FINANCIAL

Savings Deposits _____

Other Investments _____

Insurance (other than car) _____

Debt & Loan Repayments (other than car) _____

Credit Card payment _____

Loans _____

Other _____

TOTAL EXPENSES _____

MONTHLY INCOME & EXPENSES WORKSHEET

AVAILABLE INCOME (AI)

Wages and Tips _____

From Savings _____

Financial Aid (loans, grants, scholarships) _____

Parents _____

Other _____

TOTAL AI _____

TITHE & TAXES (T&T)

Tithe _____

Taxes (including taxes withheld) _____

TOTAL T&T _____

NET SPENDABLE INCOME (NSI) _____

EXPENSES
HOUSING

Rent _____

Utilities _____

Telephone _____

Furniture & Appliances _____

Other _____

FOOD

Meal Plan _____

Groceries _____

TRANSPORTATION

Car Payment _____

Car Insurance _____

Gas & Oil _____

Car Repairs _____

Public Transit _____

Other _____

EDUCATION

Tuition & Fees _____

Lab Fees _____

Other Fees _____

Books _____

MEDICAL

Doctor _____

Dentist _____

Prescriptions _____

Other _____

OTHER LIVING EXPENSES

Clothing _____

Laundry _____

Household Supplies _____

Personal Care (toiletries, hair cut/care) _____

Entertainment (dining, movies, events) _____

Gifts _____

Monthly Dues _____

Misc. Expenses _____

FINANCIAL

Savings Deposits _____

Other Investments _____

Insurance (other than car) _____

Debt & Loan Repayments (other than car) _____

Credit Card payment _____

Loans _____

Other _____

TOTAL EXPENSES _____

MONTHLY INCOME & EXPENSES WORKSHEET

AVAILABLE INCOME (AI)

Wages and Tips _____

From Savings _____

Financial Aid (loans, grants, scholarships) _____

Parents _____

Other _____

TOTAL AI _____

TITHE & TAXES (T&T)

Tithe _____

Taxes (including taxes withheld) _____

TOTAL T&T _____

NET SPENDABLE INCOME (NSI) _____

EXPENSES

HOUSING

Rent _____

Utilities _____

Telephone _____

Furniture & Appliances _____

Other _____

FOOD

Meal Plan _____

Groceries _____

TRANSPORTATION

Car Payment _____

Car Insurance _____

Gas & Oil _____

Car Repairs _____

Public Transit _____

Other _____

EDUCATION

Tuition & Fees _____

Lab Fees _____

Other Fees _____

Books _____

MEDICAL

Doctor _____

Dentist _____

Prescriptions _____

Other _____

OTHER LIVING EXPENSES

Clothing _____

Laundry _____

Household Supplies _____

Personal Care (toiletries, hair cut/care) _____

Entertainment (dining, movies, events) _____

Gifts _____

Monthly Dues _____

Misc. Expenses _____

FINANCIAL

Savings Deposits _____

Other Investments _____

Insurance (other than car) _____

Debt & Loan Repayments (other than car) _____

Credit Card payment _____

Loans _____

Other _____

TOTAL EXPENSES _____

MONTHLY INCOME & EXPENSES WORKSHEET

AVAILABLE INCOME (AI)

Wages and Tips _____

From Savings _____

Financial Aid (loans, grants, scholarships) _____

Parents _____

Other _____

TOTAL AI _____

TITHE & TAXES (T&T)

Tithe _____

Taxes (including taxes withheld) _____

TOTAL T&T _____

NET SPENDABLE INCOME (NSI) _____

EXPENSES
HOUSING

Rent _____

Utilities _____

Telephone _____

Furniture & Appliances _____

Other _____

FOOD

Meal Plan _____

Groceries _____

TRANSPORTATION

Car Payment _____

Car Insurance _____

Gas & Oil _____

Car Repairs _____

Public Transit _____

Other _____

EDUCATION

Tuition & Fees _____

Lab Fees _____

Other Fees _____

Books _____

MEDICAL

Doctor _____

Dentist _____

Prescriptions _____

Other _____

OTHER LIVING EXPENSES

Clothing _____

Laundry _____

Household Supplies _____

Personal Care (toiletries, hair cut/care) _____

Entertainment (dining, movies, events) _____

Gifts _____

Monthly Dues _____

Misc. Expenses _____

FINANCIAL

Savings Deposits _____

Other Investments _____

Insurance (other than car) _____

Debt & Loan Repayments (other than car) _____

Credit Card payment _____

Loans _____

Other _____

TOTAL EXPENSES _____

MONTHLY INCOME & EXPENSES WORKSHEET

AVAILABLE INCOME (AI)

Wages and Tips _____

From Savings _____

Financial Aid (loans, grants, scholarships) _____

Parents _____

Other _____

TOTAL AI _____

TITHE & TAXES (T&T)

Tithe _____

Taxes (including taxes withheld) _____

TOTAL T&T _____

NET SPENDABLE INCOME (NSI) _____

EXPENSES

HOUSING

Rent _____

Utilities _____

Telephone _____

Furniture & Appliances _____

Other _____

FOOD

Meal Plan _____

Groceries _____

TRANSPORTATION

Car Payment _____

Car Insurance _____

Gas & Oil _____

Car Repairs _____

Public Transit _____

Other _____

EDUCATION

Tuition & Fees _____

Lab Fees _____

Other Fees _____

Books _____

MEDICAL

Doctor _____

Dentist _____

Prescriptions _____

Other _____

OTHER LIVING EXPENSES

Clothing _____

Laundry _____

Household Supplies _____

Personal Care (toiletries, hair cut/care) _____

Entertainment (dining, movies, events) _____

Gifts _____

Monthly Dues _____

Misc. Expenses _____

FINANCIAL

Savings Deposits _____

Other Investments _____

Insurance (other than car) _____

Debt & Loan Repayments (other than car) _____

Credit Card payment _____

Loans _____

Other _____

TOTAL EXPENSES _____

MONTHLY INCOME & EXPENSES WORKSHEET

AVAILABLE INCOME (AI)

Wages and Tips _____

From Savings _____

Financial Aid (loans, grants, scholarships) _____

Parents _____

Other _____

TOTAL AI _____

TITHE & TAXES (T&T)

Tithe _____

Taxes (including taxes withheld) _____

TOTAL T&T _____

NET SPENDABLE INCOME (NSI) _____

EXPENSES

HOUSING

Rent _____

Utilities _____

Telephone _____

Furniture & Appliances _____

Other _____

FOOD

Meal Plan _____

Groceries _____

TRANSPORTATION

Car Payment _____

Car Insurance _____

Gas & Oil _____

Car Repairs _____

Public Transit _____

Other _____

EDUCATION

Tuition & Fees _____

Lab Fees _____

Other Fees _____

Books _____

MEDICAL

Doctor _____

Dentist _____

Prescriptions _____

Other _____

OTHER LIVING EXPENSES

Clothing _____

Laundry _____

Household Supplies _____

Personal Care (toiletries, hair cut/care) _____

Entertainment (dining, movies, events) _____

Gifts _____

Monthly Dues _____

Misc. Expenses _____

FINANCIAL

Savings Deposits _____

Other Investments _____

Insurance (other than car) _____

Debt & Loan Repayments (other than car) _____

Credit Card payment _____

Loans _____

Other _____

TOTAL EXPENSES _____

MONTHLY INCOME & EXPENSES WORKSHEET

AVAILABLE INCOME (AI)

Wages and Tips _____

From Savings _____

Financial Aid (loans, grants, scholarships) _____

Parents _____

Other _____

TOTAL AI _____

TITHE & TAXES (T&T)

Tithe _____

Taxes (including taxes withheld) _____

TOTAL T&T _____

NET SPENDABLE INCOME (NSI) _____

EXPENSES

HOUSING

Rent _____

Utilities _____

Telephone _____

Furniture & Appliances _____

Other _____

FOOD

Meal Plan _____

Groceries _____

TRANSPORTATION

Car Payment _____

Car Insurance _____

Gas & Oil _____

Car Repairs _____

Public Transit _____

Other _____

EDUCATION

Tuition & Fees _____

Lab Fees _____

Other Fees _____

Books _____

MEDICAL

Doctor _____

Dentist _____

Prescriptions _____

Other _____

OTHER LIVING EXPENSES

Clothing _____

Laundry _____

Household Supplies _____

Personal Care (toiletries, hair cut/care) _____

Entertainment (dining, movies, events) _____

Gifts _____

Monthly Dues _____

Misc. Expenses _____

FINANCIAL

Savings Deposits _____

Other Investments _____

Insurance (other than car) _____

Debt & Loan Repayments (other than car) _____

Credit Card payment _____

Loans _____

Other _____

TOTAL EXPENSES _____

MONTHLY INCOME & EXPENSES WORKSHEET

AVAILABLE INCOME (AI)

Wages and Tips _____

From Savings _____

Financial Aid (loans, grants, scholarships) _____

Parents _____

Other _____

TOTAL AI _____

TITHE & TAXES (T&T)

Tithe _____

Taxes (including taxes withheld) _____

TOTAL T&T _____

NET SPENDABLE INCOME (NSI) _____

EXPENSES

HOUSING

Rent _____

Utilities _____

Telephone _____

Furniture & Appliances _____

Other _____

FOOD

Meal Plan _____

Groceries _____

TRANSPORTATION

Car Payment _____

Car Insurance _____

Gas & Oil _____

Car Repairs _____

Public Transit _____

Other _____

EDUCATION

Tuition & Fees _____

Lab Fees _____

Other Fees _____

Books _____

MEDICAL

Doctor _____

Dentist _____

Prescriptions _____

Other _____

OTHER LIVING EXPENSES

Clothing _____

Laundry _____

Household Supplies _____

Personal Care (toiletries, hair cut/care) _____

Entertainment (dining, movies, events) _____

Gifts _____

Monthly Dues _____

Misc. Expenses _____

FINANCIAL

Savings Deposits _____

Other Investments _____

Insurance (other than car) _____

Debt & Loan Repayments (other than car) _____

Credit Card payment _____

Loans _____

Other _____

TOTAL EXPENSES _____

MONTHLY INCOME & EXPENSES WORKSHEET

AVAILABLE INCOME (AI)

Wages and Tips _____

From Savings _____

Financial Aid (loans, grants, scholarships) _____

Parents _____

Other _____

TOTAL AI _____

TITHE & TAXES (T&T)

Tithe _____

Taxes (including taxes withheld) _____

TOTAL T&T _____

NET SPENDABLE INCOME (NSI) _____

EXPENSES

HOUSING

Rent _____

Utilities _____

Telephone _____

Furniture & Appliances _____

Other _____

FOOD

Meal Plan _____

Groceries _____

TRANSPORTATION

Car Payment _____

Car Insurance _____

Gas & Oil _____

Car Repairs _____

Public Transit _____

Other _____

EDUCATION

Tuition & Fees _____

Lab Fees _____

Other Fees _____

Books _____

MEDICAL

Doctor _____

Dentist _____

Prescriptions _____

Other _____

OTHER LIVING EXPENSES

Clothing _____

Laundry _____

Household Supplies _____

Personal Care (toiletries, hair cut/care) _____

Entertainment (dining, movies, events) _____

Gifts _____

Monthly Dues _____

Misc. Expenses _____

FINANCIAL

Savings Deposits _____

Other Investments _____

Insurance (other than car) _____

Debt & Loan Repayments (other than car) _____

Credit Card payment _____

Loans _____

Other _____

TOTAL EXPENSES _____

MONTHLY INCOME & EXPENSES WORKSHEET

AVAILABLE INCOME (AI)

Wages and Tips   _____

From Savings   _____

Financial Aid (loans, grants, scholarships)   _____

Parents   _____

Other   _____

TOTAL AI   _____

TITHE & TAXES (T&T)

Tithe   _____

Taxes (including taxes withheld)   _____

TOTAL T&T   _____

NET SPENDABLE INCOME (NSI)   _____

EXPENSES

HOUSING

Rent   _____

Utilities   _____

Telephone   _____

Furniture & Appliances   _____

Other   _____

FOOD

Meal Plan   _____

Groceries   _____

TRANSPORTATION

Car Payment   _____

Car Insurance   _____

Gas & Oil   _____

Car Repairs   _____

Public Transit   _____

Other   _____

EDUCATION

Tuition & Fees   _____

Lab Fees   _____

Other Fees   _____

Books   _____

MEDICAL

Doctor   _____

Dentist   _____

Prescriptions   _____

Other   _____

OTHER LIVING EXPENSES

Clothing   _____

Laundry   _____

Household Supplies   _____

Personal Care (toiletries, hair cut/care)   _____

Entertainment (dining, movies, events)   _____

Gifts   _____

Monthly Dues   _____

Misc. Expenses   _____

FINANCIAL

Savings Deposits   _____

Other Investments   _____

Insurance (other than car)   _____

Debt & Loan Repayments (other than car)   _____

Credit Card payment   _____

Loans   _____

Other   _____

TOTAL EXPENSES   _____

MONTHLY INCOME & EXPENSES WORKSHEET

AVAILABLE INCOME (AI)

Wages and Tips _____

From Savings _____

Financial Aid (loans, grants, scholarships) _____

Parents _____

Other _____

TOTAL AI _____

TITHE & TAXES (T&T)

Tithe _____

Taxes (including taxes withheld) _____

TOTAL T&T _____

NET SPENDABLE INCOME (NSI) _____

EXPENSES

HOUSING

Rent _____

Utilities _____

Telephone _____

Furniture & Appliances _____

Other _____

FOOD

Meal Plan _____

Groceries _____

TRANSPORTATION

Car Payment _____

Car Insurance _____

Gas & Oil _____

Car Repairs _____

Public Transit _____

Other _____

EDUCATION

Tuition & Fees _____

Lab Fees _____

Other Fees _____

Books _____

MEDICAL

Doctor _____

Dentist _____

Prescriptions _____

Other _____

OTHER LIVING EXPENSES

Clothing _____

Laundry _____

Household Supplies _____

Personal Care (toiletries, hair cut/care) _____

Entertainment (dining, movies, events) _____

Gifts _____

Monthly Dues _____

Misc. Expenses _____

FINANCIAL

Savings Deposits _____

Other Investments _____

Insurance (other than car) _____

Debt & Loan Repayments (other than car) _____

Credit Card payment _____

Loans _____

Other _____

TOTAL EXPENSES _____

MONTHLY INCOME & EXPENSES WORKSHEET

AVAILABLE INCOME (AI)

Wages and Tips _____

From Savings _____

Financial Aid (loans, grants, scholarships) _____

Parents _____

Other _____

TOTAL AI _____

TITHE & TAXES (T&T)

Tithe _____

Taxes (including taxes withheld) _____

TOTAL T&T _____

NET SPENDABLE INCOME (NSI) _____

EXPENSES

HOUSING

Rent _____

Utilities _____

Telephone _____

Furniture & Appliances _____

Other _____

FOOD

Meal Plan _____

Groceries _____

TRANSPORTATION

Car Payment _____

Car Insurance _____

Gas & Oil _____

Car Repairs _____

Public Transit _____

Other _____

EDUCATION

Tuition & Fees _____

Lab Fees _____

Other Fees _____

Books _____

MEDICAL

Doctor _____

Dentist _____

Prescriptions _____

Other _____

OTHER LIVING EXPENSES

Clothing _____

Laundry _____

Household Supplies _____

Personal Care (toiletries, hair cut/care) _____

Entertainment (dining, movies, events) _____

Gifts _____

Monthly Dues _____

Misc. Expenses _____

FINANCIAL

Savings Deposits _____

Other Investments _____

Insurance (other than car) _____

Debt & Loan Repayments (other than car) _____

Credit Card payment _____

Loans _____

Other _____

TOTAL EXPENSES _____

MONTHLY INCOME & EXPENSES WORKSHEET

AVAILABLE INCOME (AI)

Wages and Tips _____

From Savings _____

Financial Aid (loans, grants, scholarships) _____

Parents _____

Other _____

TOTAL AI _____

TITHE & TAXES (T&T)

Tithe _____

Taxes (including taxes withheld) _____

TOTAL T&T _____

NET SPENDABLE INCOME (NSI) _____

EXPENSES

HOUSING

Rent _____

Utilities _____

Telephone _____

Furniture & Appliances _____

Other _____

FOOD

Meal Plan _____

Groceries _____

TRANSPORTATION

Car Payment _____

Car Insurance _____

Gas & Oil _____

Car Repairs _____

Public Transit _____

Other _____

EDUCATION

Tuition & Fees _____

Lab Fees _____

Other Fees _____

Books _____

MEDICAL

Doctor _____

Dentist _____

Prescriptions _____

Other _____

OTHER LIVING EXPENSES

Clothing _____

Laundry _____

Household Supplies _____

Personal Care (toiletries, hair cut/care) _____

Entertainment (dining, movies, events) _____

Gifts _____

Monthly Dues _____

Misc. Expenses _____

FINANCIAL

Savings Deposits _____

Other Investments _____

Insurance (other than car) _____

Debt & Loan Repayments (other than car) _____

Credit Card payment _____

Loans _____

Other _____

TOTAL EXPENSES _____

INDIVIDUAL CATEGORY LEDGER

				$				$	
	EXPENSE CATEGORY			ALLOCATION				ALLOCATION	

DATE	TRANSACTION	DEPOSIT		WITHDRAWAL		BALANCE	

INDIVIDUAL CATEGORY LEDGER

_____ $ _____ $ _____
EXPENSE CATEGORY   ALLOCATION   ALLOCATION

DATE	TRANSACTION	DEPOSIT		WITHDRAWAL		BALANCE	

INDIVIDUAL CATEGORY LEDGER

_____ $ _____ $ _____
EXPENSE CATEGORY   ALLOCATION   ALLOCATION

DATE	TRANSACTION	DEPOSIT	WITHDRAWAL	BALANCE	

INDIVIDUAL CATEGORY LEDGER

		$		$	
	EXPENSE CATEGORY	ALLOCATION		ALLOCATION	

DATE	TRANSACTION	DEPOSIT		WITHDRAWAL		BALANCE	

INDIVIDUAL CATEGORY LEDGER

	EXPENSE CATEGORY	$ ALLOCATION	$ ALLOCATION

DATE	TRANSACTION	DEPOSIT	WITHDRAWAL	BALANCE	

INDIVIDUAL CATEGORY LEDGER

_____ $ _____ $ _____

EXPENSE CATEGORY   ALLOCATION   ALLOCATION

DATE	TRANSACTION	DEPOSIT	WITHDRAWAL	BALANCE

INDIVIDUAL CATEGORY LEDGER

_____ $ _____ $ _____
EXPENSE CATEGORY   ALLOCATION   ALLOCATION

DATE	TRANSACTION	DEPOSIT		WITHDRAWAL		BALANCE	

INDIVIDUAL CATEGORY LEDGER

	$		$	
EXPENSE CATEGORY	ALLOCATION		ALLOCATION	

DATE	TRANSACTION	DEPOSIT		WITHDRAWAL		BALANCE	

INDIVIDUAL CATEGORY LEDGER

$ _____ $ _____

EXPENSE CATEGORY   ALLOCATION   ALLOCATION

DATE	TRANSACTION	DEPOSIT		WITHDRAWAL		BALANCE	

INDIVIDUAL CATEGORY LEDGER

EXPENSE CATEGORY		$ _____ ALLOCATION		$ _____ ALLOCATION

DATE	TRANSACTION	DEPOSIT	WITHDRAWAL	BALANCE

INDIVIDUAL CATEGORY LEDGER

		$		
	EXPENSE CATEGORY	ALLOCATION	$ ALLOCATION	

DATE	TRANSACTION	DEPOSIT	WITHDRAWAL	BALANCE

INDIVIDUAL CATEGORY LEDGER

		$		$	
EXPENSE CATEGORY		ALLOCATION		ALLOCATION	

DATE	TRANSACTION	DEPOSIT		WITHDRAWAL		BALANCE	